POEMS BY GERALD BULLETT

ALSO BY GERALD BULLETT

THE GOLDEN YEAR OF FAN CHENG-TA
WINTER SOLSTICE
POEMS IN PENCIL
THE BUBBLE
GEORGE ELIOT: HER LIFE AND BOOKS
THE TESTAMENT OF LIGHT
THE ENGLISH GALAXY OF SHORTER POEMS

and many novels

POEMS

BY

GERALD BULLETT

CAMBRIDGE
AT THE UNIVERSITY PRESS
1949

CAMBRIDGE
UNIVERSITY PRESS

University Printing House, Cambridge CB2 8BS, United Kingdom

Cambridge University Press is part of the University of Cambridge.

It furthers the University's mission by disseminating knowledge in the pursuit of education, learning and research at the highest international levels of excellence.

www.cambridge.org
Information on this title: www.cambridge.org/9781107554283

First published 1949
First paperback edition 2015

A catalogue record for this publication is available from the British Library

ISBN 978-1-107-55428-3 Paperback

Twenty-five of these thirty-six poems now appear for the first time in book form: they have been written, at very irregular intervals, during the past ten or twelve years. The rest are selected from previous volumes: *Poems in Pencil* (Dent, 1937) and *Winter Solstice* (Cambridge University Press, 1943). The sixty stanzas from the Chinese entitled *The Golden Year of Fan Cheng-ta* (Cambridge, 1946) are not represented here, because they form a natural sequence and are in effect one poem.

G. B.

CONTENTS

NEW POEMS

POEMS IN PENCIL

WINTER SOLSTICE

NEW POEMS

THE CHILD

Where now is the child
  Who at morning prime
Watched in its first unfolding
  The flower of time:

Saw with astonisht eyes,
  In secrecy, alone,
Open upon a virgin world
  The petals of the sun:

With curious fingers
  Touched the living grass,
Warm with glow of the dandelion,
  The first that was:

Upon what pillow,
  Under my fleece of years
From sight and hearing buried,
  Breathes he, and stirs?

MORNING GLORY

The water sparkles as I pour,
Each drop a crystal gem,
Each several drop a gleaming world
Lost in the clear containing glass
Or in the basin lying sleek and still.
What richness!—when a man may slake
His sleepy thirst with precious gems,
And among shining planets plunge his hands.

APRIL EVENING

O sadness of evening
  In April, when the sun
Has gone away, leaving
  The garden all alone
And the dim-lit faces
  Of daffodils astare,
Witless and beautiful,
  As innocents are.

O sadness remembering
  The unfolding buds
Of an earlier April
  Now fallen into dust,
And the stilled voices,
  And the bright eyes
Darken'd, and the vanisht
  Individual fragrances.

O sadness, O beauty,
  O birds that call
Placidly one to another,
  Till darkness fall.
O lovely perishable lives
  Of leaf and flower,
Growing and knowing not
  How brief your hour.

TO A HEDGEHOG

And did the unwonted sun
  This winter morning,
Illusionary glow
  Of spring's returning,

Did the sun's quickness
  So stir your blood,
From shadowy hedge and green verge
  You needs must seek the road?

My two hands lifted you,
  You bequill'd and curl'd
Into the brown semblance
  Of a prickly world.

My two hands turned you over,
  My curious eyes
Stared at the strange secret
  They could not surprise,

Stared at the sharp beseeching face,
  The red mouth mute,
Marvelling that one so midget-small
  Should wear so huge a coat,

Or, having put it on,
Should through the centuries
Have learnt so little
The logic of disguise

As here to wander,
In sight of all who pass,
Far from confusing cover
Or tall grass.

Dim is your light, traveller,
Your goal obscure:
Man's searching wit, of mine,
Can tell no more.

Strangers and brothers so,
We stare, you and I.
Strangers and fellow-pilgrims,
We live and we die.
There's no knowing why.

PROTEUS

Into your home, to find a fallen crumb,
Mousing my way on velvet feet I come.
Brilliant as flame, sleek as water's flow,
I, panther, sinuously come and go.
Serpent or toad or cold chameleon,
I seek my swamp, or bake me in the sun,
Or blithely sing, a blackbird on the bough,
Not past nor future time, but here and now.
Rooted in dark, beyond sound or sight,
I lift my leafy branches to the light.
I am earth, air, fire, water, rising sap.
Nothing contains me. I escape your trap.

THE LOOKING-GLASS

I met an old woman
  adrift in the rain
Under the hedge
  at turn of the lane.
I asked her civilly
  how she did.
'Lord a mercy,
  I'm lost,' she said.

'Yesterday morning
  as ever was,
Honey and roses
  I see in the glass,
Honey and roses
  and raven hair,
In the looking-glass
  a-top of my stair.

'Yesterday's gone,
  and now today
The one that looks out
  is lean and grey.
What ails my eyes
  no longer to see
In my looking-glass
  the girl I be?'

MOLEHILL

These grasses, that were once a level lawn
And now so rank and mettlesome are grown,
With ragwort plantain thistle seeding dock
Give up their ghosts under my lethal hook.

And here, halfway across the wilderland,
There's new-till'd earth, a neat and modest mound,
To mark where lives a self-invited guest,
His secret innocently manifest.

He buries him alive, resolved to shun
The loud light, the violence of the sun,
Nor blithe descanting bird nor summer's bloom
Can tempt him from his residential tomb.

I leave him there to enjoy his dark day,
Contrive no trap his dullness to betray.
Some a more genial neighbour may prefer,
But no one could demand a quieter.

CATTLE MARKET

In market-square attend their turn for sale
Bullock and heifer, tether'd nose to rail,
And murmuring yoe, and bleating newborn lamb,
And long-eared calfling mouthing at his dam.
Whether such merchandise some doubts may feel,
Or marketable lots, of beef and veal,
Have wit enough to wonder what's to come
And wish themselves at home,
Recalling—while men move among their ranks
To prod appraisingly their velvet flanks—
The green pastures, the cool
Long draught from running brook or shaded pool,
We do not care to know.
Rather, while these our brothers come and go,
Ourselves with hearts averse and hurrying feet
Pass by them lest they greet us—lest they greet
With loving looks and uncomplaining prayers
The eyes of their betrayers.

THE CHESTNUT TREE

My chestnut tree, the summer through,
He showed so little change of hue
His green composure made me feel
That time, as well as he, stood still.
But when September's burning days
Had spilled their sun and gone their ways,
It was for all the world as if
His leaves were fashion'd of gold leaf.

Now days grow short. The ageing year
Turns green and gold to brown and sere.
And still my chestnut, since he must,
Stands splendid in his robes of rust.
The garden 's bare of fruit and flower,
The mute birds sadden, hour by hour:
Yet I could stand all day and browse
Among these pendent folios.

Here on this copious crispy head
The sun's diurnal round I read,
To find inscrolled on his last page
Bright emblem of a golden age:
For when the day grows red and dim,
And the sun rests on the world's rim,
My tree, lit by that flaming rose,
How like a lamp he burns and glows!

THE APPARITION

Home coming, in the narrow verge between
Daylight and dusk, the sky a lucent green,
Mid long-familiar fields and ways well known,
We found ourselves in a strange land, alone.

Our voices, in the bland October air
Dissolving, seemed to come from otherwhere.
Footsteps, like pebbles dropt in a still pool,
Made the pervading stillness palpable.

We thought ourselves alone, in all the land
No other soul, till suddenly, near at hand,
Ruddy and gold the great orb of the moon
Leaned on the hedge and lookt us up and down.

THE WISH

I watched my father plant a maiden beech,
Her highest tapering twig within my reach:
I watched him tread, to make it firm and trim,
The broken ground that soon must cover him.

I asked him if in long or little time
The sapling would be big enough to climb.
House-high, he teased, tomorrow she would grow:
I only wished it could be sooner so.

And now tomorrow's come, and I, a man,
Past the meridian of my mortal span,
Stare at these mighty branches in dismay
And fondly wish today were yesterday.

A STILL MORNING

In March, on a still morning,
Motionless and bare
Stand the seven tall trees,
Alive in the cool air.

The slight, pencilling shadows,
The pale gold of the sun's
Lantern glow, move
Unperceivably on.

The light may quiver,
The clear blue of the sky,
Ground of their tracery,
Tremble as with joy,

But the seven tall trees,
Like a celestial thought
Conceived in stillness,
Stand, and stir not.

They stand in a bright silence,
Till one bird's call,
Aloft in the high bare branches,
Makes sunlight audible.

SUMMER'S END

Colours tarnisht, pride fallen, flame spent,
Majestic still in faded green and gold,
Now dying summer leaves her large intent,
And gives her leavings to enrich the mould.

October tames the tumult in the blood,
And buxom joys are put to bed again.
But sap too soon leaps in the winter'd wood
And spring returning quickens the old pain.

While page by page the process of the year
Strict audit of our small account presents,
May it not be the melancholy tear
Proves and reproves but half the evidence?

This crystal orb containing my self-love
Brings to the eye as in a convex glass
The microcosmic world in which I move,
Its suns and stars, its moon that never was:

Held for a moment, luminously bright,
It lingers on the lashes, thence to fall,
In chine of cheek losing its shatter'd light,
As must at last the lantern of my skull.

Each in his hour, a lighted skeleton,
Knowing nor whence nor whither, nor what spark

Kindled the incandescence of the bone,
We go our devious ways from dark to dark.

Like leaves we rust, like leaves we grow to grief,
Our dreaming earth to earth reluctant give.
So be it, so the life that lived the leaf
Has other leaves and other lives to live:

For as this giant oak whose limbs we climb,
Each in our generation, sire and son,
Holds here within his huge embrace of time
Unnumber'd store of golden moments gone,

With all he was and all he is become,
The buried seed, the many-branching tower:
So, I that am when I am not shall sum
All summers, and all seasons, in an hour.

Yet still the moving year my heart misgives,
Autumnal odours breathe of summer slain,
Stark winter's quilting covers up her leaves,
And spring returning quickens the old pain:

Quickens the pulse, makes green the sullen wood,
And, winter's brood of caution put to flight,
Sets dancing in the clear flame of the blood
Intolerable dreams of dear delight,

New ghosts of old desire.

CHRISTMAS ROSE

Wing'd blossom of white thought, yellow-centred
Star of fertility sprung from December soil,
Six perfect petal-rays of frozen light:

See, under the stark oak, in her nest
Of long, serrated, green, environing leaves,
Where like a bird she listens and looks out,

See now, at twilight, how her pale presence,
Even between sundown and dawning star,
Fills the dusk with quickness, quiet as prayer.

A DAY IN NOVEMBER

By misty fields and water-falling boughs
Along a sodden path we picked our way,
Wondering why we'd left our dry house
To look for kindle-wood on such a day,
With summer gone and autumn in collapse,
Nothing to see, and nothing much to say:
So came at last to a three-cornered copse
Where there was wood in plenty. We didn't mind
That every leaf was laced with water-drops,
For it wasn't leafy boughs we'd come to find,
But sticks: dried fingers that would snap
At a touch from our live ones: that's the kind.
The branchlet you can bend is full of sap,
All such we left growing their own ways
To bear a brood of young leaves in the lap
Of a remote season's merrier days.
Loitering homeward late in the afternoon
We warmed our musing fancy in the blaze
That on our hearth would leap and crackle soon,
Making a third to spend the evening with.
The memory's like an idle murmuring tune,
The day's savour subtle and fugitive.
You'd hardly, I imagine, call it pleasure:
Merely a quiet sense of being together.

TO TSUI CHI

When I remember you, my friend Tsui Chi,
I remember the genial ghost who came with you,
In silken robe, venerably bearded,
Poet and elder brother Fan Cheng-ta:
In whose serene mind one summer's day
We lived and sunned ourselves, hardly knowing
Whether the arc of sky bending above us
Shed its delight on Sussex or Soochow.
I remember too, from an earlier millenium,
Chang Tai-kung, most courteous of anglers,
Who with unbaited line in a golden river
Clear-flowing as his charitable dream
Sat fishing all day long,
Inviting, but unwilling to constrain
With worm or hook, his brethren from the water.
Him too you brought that summer's day: you three
Here in my garden walked and talked with me.

AFTER READING *THE TALE OF GENJI*

The fife does not suffer nor the drum have visions.
Clockwork falters, but not with melancholy.
It is strange how the chemistry of flesh and blood
Can precipitate thought, and black marks on white paper
Englobe the luminous being of dead men.
It is strange that Murasaki, who of her inwardness
Spun this web of amorous iridescence,
Can taste no more the applesharp air of spring,
Nor watch the cicada emerge from the chrysalis,
Nor, with brush poised, in an evening of meditation,
Listen for the voices of her flowering fantasy
And feel in her eyes the warm tears of Genji.
It is strange that we, and Murasaki no longer,
Can enter the world of her delicate imagining;
And strangest of all that we take the unfathomable
For commonplace truth, easy of explanation.
'Where is the wonder?' we say. 'What more natural
Than that these hieroglyphs, for our use and benefit,
Should hold the anguish and ecstasy of human hearts?'

BRIDE OF GOD

You who are going now
  Into a silent place,
Leaving with us who are left
  A deadlier silentness,

A hesitation in hearts
  Counting over the loss
Of what in your curious wisdom
  You are taking from us,

Will you remember, as we shall,
  The talk in the garden,
The birdsong and appleblossom
  Of a lost Eden?

Though he requite your love
  With holier raptures,
Must God take all you have?
  Nothing left for his creatures?

DARK IS THY LIGHT

Dark is thy light,
  in whom we live and move,
Whom seeking not we find,
  yet know not save by love:

And know not save by love
  of these our mortal kin,
These molecules of mind
  whom thou dwellest in:

These little moles of men,
  each in his earth alone,
Whom yet thou dwellest in,
  divisionless, one:

Each in our earth alone,
  dreading thy dazzling light,
Who know thee, not by knowledge,
  and see thee, not with sight.

GARDENERS

Gardeners are good. Such vices as they have
Are like the warts and bosses in the wood
Of an old oak. They're patient, stubborn folk,
As needs must be whose busyness it is
To tutor wildness, making war on weeds.
With slow sagacious words and knowing glance
They scan the sky, do all that mortals may
To learn civility to pesty birds
Come after new green peas, cosset and prune
Roses, wash with lime the orchard trees,
Make sun-parlours for seedlings.

Patient, stubborn.

Add cunning next, unless you'd put it first;
For while to dig and delve is all their text
There's cunning in their fingers to persuade
Beauty to bloom and riot to run right,
Mattock and spade, trowel and rake and hoe
Being not tools to learn by learning rules
But extra limbs these husbands of the earth
Had from their birth. Of malice they've no more
Than snaring slugs and wireworms will appease,
Or may with ease be drowned in mugs of mild.
Wherefore I say again, whether or no
It is their occupation makes them so,
Gardeners are good, in grain.

WINTER SCENES

Though steely blind the winter sky,
And summer's brag a hollow ghost,
This glancing irony of frost
Kindles a gleam in every eye.

Skating and sledging, horse and truck,
Is all our navigation now;
And, snug in ice-bound water, how
The frigid fish enjoy their luck!

Skeleton trees with gems are hung;
High fly the geese in goosely faith;
The silver cloud of our own breath
Ghostly goes with us along.

And when, too swiftly and too soon,
Day darkens, walls and glassy track
Another bounteous boon give back,
Flooding the world with milk of moon.

CHRISTMAS EVE

Red berry nor green leaf
  Nor look of any flower
These high wide spaces
  Inhabits, this bleak hour.
Glows in this solitude,
  For gay relief,
Primrose nor pimpernel,
  Red berry nor green leaf.

The timid hare lies low.
  Weasel and mouse
Keep themselves secret,
  Each in his frosty house.
The whisper of the cold
  Comes like a singing sword
Where cowers on bare branch
  A muted bird.

Yet is this deathly scene,
  This sky pale as milk,
This frozen grass that gives
  Like crackling silk,
These bare downs billowing
  Each into each,
Not dead, nor barren
  Of comfortable speech.

Here in mid winter
  Their iron sepulchre,
The seedlings of the sun
  Quicken and stir:
The holy child of love
  Wakes in his mother's womb,
Growing in quietness
  Till her time be come.

Here the divine flower
  Of natural loves,
Growing in quietness
  As a flower does,
Unfolds to ensyllable
  The creative thought,
That a new word be spoken
  And a new world wrought.

Now praise we and adore
  This majesty of birth,
Whose every frail flowering
  Brings heaven to earth,
And pray that from this hour
  In all the sons of men
Christ his living charity
  Be born again.

MOONSHINE

No dearth of sunlight, now the primrose runs
Riot on banks and scatters them with suns,
Nor moonshine while, enraptured at the sight,
The jet-enamelled blackthorn blushes white.

THE GARDEN 1945

Into this one of many worlds, defined
By elderly penmen on legal parchment,
Into this long-deserted garden
Return'd at last, I find my seedling hopes,
Hornbeam, hazel, and other penknife pilferings,
Grown to a high hedge, whence, confidingly,
Blackbird and thrush emerge with sidelong glance
To take bread of my scattering. I in fancy,
Forgetting the atom bomb, live for a moment
That small abundant life of innocent greed,
Bright-eyed, busy, unanxiously alert,
Ready to retire at the least alarm
Into the green covert.

The trees have opened broad umbrellas
For such as would gather in the dark circle.
The lawns are a labyrinthine forest
Aswarm with lives, one awareness
Looking from a million eyes, moving unmoved
In planet and plant, man and minimus,
The ant and the aphis and the plowman worm.

Here God is green, here runs and crawls and flies,
Becomes a bush, a tree, a nested bird,
Root leaf and soil, Sirius and Cassiopeia,
And staggers, ant, with load of provender,

Pushing his way among the monstrous grasses.
The sun shines; weeds prosper;
Among the glistening grasses the rain falls.
Above, the brilliant bullfinch and his wife
Weave a curving pattern
About the heads of lanky seeding groundsel,
Which, magically hovering, never alighting,
They attack with swift beaks, wings fluttering,
Then with their silken morsel dart fluently away,
Gliding to a secure foothold, to gather poise
For further flights, or vanish beyond vision
To the secret places where they have their home.

Gossips tell of tremendous perturbations:
The night-long drone of planes going and coming
Over your very bed, bombs falling
On field and farm, watchers on the downs
Patrolling under the doom of the sky's dome,
Firebombs that fell, blazing,
Here in the garden, to hiss away their existences,
Burning holes in the grass for Nature to mend,
And now become—with all such eccentricities
Deranging the rural order of days and seasons—
Already an old rumour, scarce believable.
Already the tide of time, though it were yesterday,
Erases the incredible footprint of fact,
Leaving the sand smooth for castle-building.

Here, nothing was known. The green grass,
Alive in the pulsing of its sap, enjoying
Perpetual commerce with the far-fetched sunlight,
Each blade an individual in spite of the uniform,
Went on being grass and asked no better. Trees,
Putting new leaves on bare boughs and in due season
Shedding them ungriev'd for the soil's usances,
Lived on in their own silence, enduring
The perennial cycle of sloth and urgency
For the joy unspoken, the joy unspeakable,
Of that which they are, not other than ourselves,
Though unminding and immune to our ways of being.
And undisturb'd by noise of battle above them
The ant and the beetle pursued their curious economies:
So, too, this grasshopper balancing on a blade,
This gnat, this crane-fly, this spider suddenly aware,
This slow-worm, flexible rod of metal,
Lying so still in my path
That I marvel to see the stillness change into movement,
Imperceptibly, the one flowing into the other,
As it glides like water away, to vanish in the grass.

Here no rumour runs of the dark doom
With which we threaten ourselves, we uneasily
Hesitating, between ape and angel.
Here in the garden time is an opening flower,
And Man alone is afraid.

IN THE GARDEN AT NIGHT

Be still, my soul. Consider
  The flowers and the stars.
Among these sleeping fragrances,
  Sleep now your cares.
That which the universe
  Lacks room to enclose
Lives in the folded petals
  Of this dark rose.

POEMS IN PENCIL

1937

SUDDEN SPRING

Spring is sudden: it is her quality.
However carefully we watch for her,
However long delay'd
The green in the winter'd hedge
The almond blossom
The piercing daffodil,
Like a lovely woman late for her appointment
She's suddenly here, taking us unawares,
So beautifully annihilating expectation
That we applaud her punctual arrival.

WATER

Nothing is lovelier than moving water,
The diamond element, innumerable jewel,
Brittle and splintering under the sharp sun,
Yet softer than doves' feathers, and more smooth
Than down of swan.

Nothing is lovelier than water lying still,
When the Moon takes that stillness for her glass.

WHITE FROST

I went to the window, where the morning was,
And saw innocence scatter'd on the grass.
On blade and bough it lay, on wall and gable,
Fresh with the freshness of old fable.

A blackbird on the lawn stood listening,
His orange beak glistening,
His every feather still as stone.
Such stillness, such brightness, I had never known.

Still was the garden, and, beyond,
The frosted pane of the duck-pond.
And quilted downs and distant cottages
Stood not more still than the austere trees.

Morning, new-born of a pale, virgin sky,
Found those bare trees as much surprised as I.
But though I stared and stared, and stare my fill,
They keep their secret, still.

WOODPECKER

Suddenly, like an arrow from the East,
Smart as new paint appeared our gorgeous guest,
Green in his plumage, scarlet on his crown,
Strolling about a tree-trunk upsidedown,
Tap-tapping busily with beak on bark,
His mind imagineless, his purpose dark
To us who watched him, startled out of speech,
Exchanging secret glances each with each.
So all that day, being young and fearing not
Lest custom dull the treasure we had got,
All that day long we jingled, as we went,
New-minted coins of bright astonishment.

MOORHEN

Little she knows of what may lie beyond
The verges of the pond,
Nor in that rippling glass can she descry
The moving pattern painted in the sky.
Little she knows, I think, but dumb delight
Of warm and cold, of day and dewy night,
The cool of water lapping on her breast,
And the maternal solace of the nest:
And here is all she needs.
En-islanded she broods among the reeds,
And having laid her eggs she thinks no harm
To sit alone all day and keep them warm.
When men with carts come by, or lurching cows,
Or shrieking children shake the willow-boughs,
Like formless shadows on a lighted blind
Anonymous terror moves across her mind,
And yet, for good or ill,
She's patient even so, and holds her still.
And if some wanton hand her brood destroy,
Her busy heart bereave of all its joy,
Having no wit to question or complain
That all was done in vain,
Blind to the vision moving in her blood,
Unknowing bride of God,
She'll give herself again to motherhood.

CAT AND STARLINGS

Like busy women doing chores,
Each morning to my garden come
The glossy starlings in their scores,
To fill themselves with crust and crumb.

The cat sits on the window-sill,
By me commanded, luckless beast,
Watching the hussies take their fill
And dreaming of a different feast.

The starlings look the other way,
And 'tis a grace they can't afford,
To pause before the meal and say:
'Be present at our table, Lord!'

CORN HARVEST

When round the field, where rabbits have their homes,
The rattling reaper comes
To build our harvest into tidy stooks,
There's fun for country folks.

The ambusht rabbits, pricking up their ears,
Flee the approaching shears,
And hide them deeper in such dwindling corn
As still remains unshorn.

They hide them deep, with mouse and nestling vole,
But every silly soul,
Each filament of fur from nose to scut
Aware of what's afoot,

Will soon or late his scanty refuge yield,
And brave the stubble-field.
Then shouts go up. With rabbit on the run
The jolly game's begun.

With stones and staves we head him off from home
And hunt him to his doom,
Men women children, noisy with good will,
All crowding to the kill:

Nor pause we in our muddy mirth to scan
Our own contracting span,
And mark, while Fate with viewless engine nears,
The rattle of the shears.

MAN AND HARE

I stopt the car. Herself, with sidelong look,
Sat in the lighted circle, ears a-cock.
Like harvest moons new fallen from the sky
My headlamps must have seemed to her slant eye:
In whose warm skin, seeing them so, I sat,
And wondered what the world would now be at.

THE EXILE

In the dead middle of night,
Quiet and cold,
I heard the screwk of Chantecleer:
Three times he called.
It was an angry signature
Upon the silence scrawled.

Thrice at the frozen hour
He cried his crow,
Waking from dreams of what he was
Milleniums ago,
When, in forests of India,
Under a royal sun,
He with his wives, many and meek,
Lived like Solomon.

Some vestiges remain
Of dreams so deep:
Round his insulted heart
Sick humours creep:
And with his crooked crow he signs
The death-warrant of sleep.

THE ROSE

Though from faded leaf
The dark flower fall,
Her burning all too brief
That seemed perpetual,

And, while scent lingers,
The rose-petals dim
Crumble in the fingers
That would gather them,

Her fair body broken
Petal by petal and gone,
Here, with no token,
The Rose blooms on.

WINTER SOLSTICE

1943

Be wary that thou conceive not bodily that which
is meant ghostly, although it be spoken
in bodily words, as be these.

THE CLOUD OF UNKNOWING

I

In secret, in the all-creative silence,
Behind the mask, under the crust of winter,
Love lives unmanifest, pain stirs,
Desire cries in the night unappeasable.
Unappeasable the isolated spirit
Waking alone, the self in the seed,
The minute particle, the bubble ego,
Waking alone to its own aloneness:
Till, in the appointed season,
As it were sunseeds sepulchred in earth
And from that tomb
Leaping to communion with their parent light,
Love, longing beyond mortal measure,
Breaks into flower and leaf.
                                        Spirit knows
Its own: in the multitudinous illusion
Of time, in its own myriad imaginings
Incarnate, the eternal seeks and finds itself:
In earth air fire water, beast and bird,
Beetle and bug and mayfly, all that inhabits
Day's wide welkin, bowl of abundancy,
Or sky of sable bursting into coruscation
Of moon and stars.
                                In the lithe tracery
Of bare trees on winter's callow sky,

In bird flying, frog spawning, gelid fish
Cosily pillowed in cold shadow under
The thin pane of the pond my window looks on,
In the hieroglyph of heaven, the vein'd leaf,
The cosmic phantasy and the microcosmic
Spirit of man, moved to infinite desire and
Dark with the shadow of doom long foreknown,
There runs the signature of a nameless mystery
Too near for knowledge and too far for finding,
Save in the wordless motions of the heart.
Curt ecstasy, bitter fulfilment,
Wounding wonder of dissevered union,
When every moment's marriage of true hearts
Involves its own divorce, which hands and lips,
Fondly consenting, strive against in vain:
Such are our loves.

Brief love, because brief life. The candle's out
Ere yet the match that kindled it is cold,
And they are left to mourn whom in their turn,
And in no distant day, others must mourn for,
Shadows lamenting shadows. We emerge
As moments in a dream, for whom, momently,
The bell tolls: for whom the bell tolls.

II

Even we, the middling sedentary men,
Middling in worldly status and dignity,
Whose condition would be accounted comfort by some
And by others regarded as a hairshirt
Intolerably irksome, we whom Success,
Pre-eminent explorer of suburban avenues
And tireless turner of imperial stones,
Has never much regarded, nor we her,
Though had she more inclined herself towards us
We should not I doubt have been deterred
By her unimpeachable vulgarity
From the bosom where our betters lie buried before us:
Even we, even I, I in my middle years
Who have so far survived, with others of my age,
The two wars of our incomparable time,
Even we have known pain and fear
(Small pain, much fear, since the heart is a child)
And we understand something, though little enough,
Of the long night and the breaking heart.

I have lain a long time in the darkness of the spirit,
Hearing my own heart, and yours who suffer.
And to you, wherever you are, who sit fingering
The unanswerable letter, you who listen
For the stilled laughter, the uncoming footstep,

You patterning in time, as God knows all must,
The eternal crucifixion that is love,
To you I bring my pennyworth of pain
In brotherly token. It is all I have.

The agony of the flesh let no man belittle,
But the agony of the flesh must have an end.
The agony of the spirit is the agony or terror
Of the going out of lights, one after one.
But if you untie the hard knot of the will,
Something happens that is like a miracle.
The last star quenched, the last light gone,
The last and longest and cruellest, which is hope,
Darkness like a rose dawns at the still centre,
And the spirit is home.

It is possible that death is something like this.

I am not of those who 'know' about these things
But I have lain a long time in the darkness
And here I make report.

III

In the heart of the lotus, at the still centre,
There is peace.

Not poppied oblivion, not the dim dream,
Not the spent swimmer on the salt shore
Lying prone, not the deep repose
After perfected passion, not the luxury
Of arriving from the cold climb
At the inn and the inglenook and the spread table,
Not the drowsy pleasure
Of tiredness aching out of warm limbs,
Not folding of the hands for sleep,
Not dream, nor trance,
Not slumber nor the visitations of slumber:

Not these, but a quietness,
Wherein the senses five
In the lens of the spirit are made one,
And made alive.

IV

Now from this inwardness walled in with books
I carry my thoughts into the luminous
Wide room under the sky. On field and road,

On farm and folding downs, the sky has cast
His fleece, and mirth lies fallow with the land.
The bells of Christ are silent. Winter and war
Bring havoc to the heart: which yet believes,
So still the day with blithe expectancy,
That of the winter'd earth's long chastisement
New strength and beauty may be brought to birth
And ancient joy return,
So still the world this winter noon.

V

So still the world this winter noon,
So sparkling-cold and still,
Of quietness the heart
Could take her fill.

Upon the shallow snow
Clear rang my careful tread.
Summer had died, long ago,
But was not dead

While from the lattice thorn,
To chide my lingering doubt,
Lively with faith and fear
A feather'd eye looked out,

And on the powder'd verge,
Where road gives way to grass
For others' coming and going,
Many a printing was

Of blackbird, of wren:
Who burn away their blood,
Even as we,
To ends not understood.

So rare the fallen fleece of sky,
So far the noise of men,
Myself for a musing moment
Was blackbird, was wren.

VI

In a season of rejoicing there is much to remember
Of sadness. At the feast of friends
There are always—whether of living or dead—
Ghosts in attendance, and as time goes on,
With this or that one away, who came often, or who

Sat for many a year in the window-seat
Knitting the past into remember'd patterns,
With guests gone and children no longer children,
The ghosts come to outnumber the rest of us.
You could almost tell the years of a man's age,
The quality and measure of his heart's maturity,
By the ghosts that gather at his table
In the season of the celebration of the myth.
For unto us a child is born, unto us a son is given,
Venite adoremus dominum.

A lovely legend carries its own warrant:
But myth in the soil of a literal mind
Grows rank, taking to itself
All that else would nourish the spirit of man
Hungry for the silence of its native mystery.
Omnia exeunt in mysterium
And that alone is real which is alone
From everlasting to everlasting.
That alone is real which cannot be known,
For it is the knowing.
That alone is real which cannot be thought,
For it is the thinking.
When you came to your cradle, that was there
Which is nothing, nameless, nowhere, everywhere.

VII

Cast words away. In secret, in silence,
That which no thought can compass nor tongue tell,
The heart knows.

Too far to be found, too near to be known,
Meaning eludes our nets, the mystery
Cannot be stated. Not that words falter:
Falter they may but do not falter enough.
Even the shyest among them, the half-heard
Disavowal, hint of qualification,
Is overbold: all words are overbold:
With saying and gainsaying, myth and metaphysic,
They crowd the temple. If my words were clear
They were too clear: if cloudy, still too clear:
And, having said, I cast my words away.

Time gathers in day's eye, the things we speak
Go and are gone, fall as petals fall
Summer by summer till the doom of time
To dream desireless in the long grass,
Fade as the circling voices of the sea
Fade in the mind when the dark angel comes
With all-consuming quiet, warm and good
As honey'd hawthorn loading April air
Wave upon wave, to give our senses sleep.

From world withdrawn the inner mind awakes:
Darkness without, the lamp is lit within.
Words vanish, thought dissolves,
And from the shadowy dissolving husk
Meaning emerges, and the host is here.

VIII

Nothing, nameless, nowhere, everywhere:
When you came to your cradle I was there.
Creaturely kind in lion and lamb,
In star shining, in bud breaking, I am.
I am fear and faith, the fall and the contrition,
The aching hope and the wry fruition,
The bread of communion, the wine of bliss,
The living water of quietness,
The corn ripening, the linnet calling,
The first feathers of dusk falling,
The comrade, the lover, the casual friend.
I am that you shall find at the day's end.

For EU product safety concerns, contact us at Calle de José Abascal, 56–1°,
28003 Madrid, Spain or eugpsr@cambridge.org.

www.ingramcontent.com/pod-product-compliance
Ingram Content Group UK Ltd.
Pitfield, Milton Keynes, MK11 3LW, UK
UKHW012334130625
459647UK00009B/275